New N Word documents

Run the macro:
```
Sub New_N_document()
' New_N_document Macro
'In example N=7

For i = 1 To 7
    Documents.Add
DocumentType:=wdNewBlankDocument
Next i

End Sub
```

	You can change a number in red circle (below). It means how many new documents will be open.

```
Sub New_N_document()
' New_N_document Macro
'In example N=7

For i = 1 To (7)
    Documents.Add DocumentType:=wdNewBlankDocument
Next i

End Sub
```

Close the document

Run the macro:
```
Sub Close_the_document()
'
' Close_the_document Macro
'
    ActiveWindow.Close
End Sub
```

	If the document contains unsaved changes, the save window will appear.

Select all document content

Run the macro:
```
Sub Select_All_Document_Content()
'
' Select_All_Document_Content Macro
'
    Selection.WholeStory
End Sub
```

Apply bold formatting to text

Run the macro:
```
Sub Apply_Bold_Formatting_To_Text()
'
' Apply_Bold_Formatting_To_Text Macro
'
    Selection.Font.Bold = wdToggle
End Sub
```

	If text was previously selected, the change will be applied to it. The change will also be applied to any text that was written after running the macro.
	If no text was previously selected, the change will only be applied to the text that was written when the macro was run.
	If the **Bold** attribute was enabled, running the macro will disable it.

Apply italic formatting to text

Run the macro:
```
Sub Apply_Italic_Formatting_To_Text()
'
```

```
' Apply_Italic_Formatting_To_Text Macro
'

    Selection.Font.Italic = wdToggle
End Sub
```

→	If text was previously selected, the change will be applied to it. The change will also be applied to any text that was written after running the macro.
→	If no text was previously selected, the change will only be applied to the text that was written when the macro was run.
→	If the **Italic** attribute was enabled, running the macro will disable it.

Apply underline formatting to text

Run the macro:
```
Sub Apply_Underline_Formatting_To_Text()
'

' Apply_Underline_Formatting_To_Text
Macro
'
'

    If Selection.Font.Underline =
wdUnderlineNone Then
        Selection.Font.Underline =
wdUnderlineSingle
    Else
        Selection.Font.Underline =
wdUnderlineNone
    End If
End Sub
```

→	If text was previously selected, the change will be applied to it. The change will also be applied to any text that was written after running the macro.
→	If no text was previously selected, the change will only be applied to the text that was written when the

	macro was run.
⇨	If the **Uderline** attribute was enabled, running the macro will disable it.

Apply underline single formatting to text

Run the macro:

```
Sub Apply_Underline_Formatting_To_Text1()
'
' Apply_Underline_Formatting_To_Text1
Macro
'
    Selection.Font.Underline =
wdUnderlineSingle
End Sub
```

Change font attributes

Run the macro:

```
Sub Change_Font_Attributes()
'
' Change_Font_Attributes Macro
'
'
    With Selection.Font
        .Name = "Algerian"
        .Size = 11
        .Bold = False
        .Italic = False
        .Underline = wdUnderlineNone
        .UnderlineColor =
wdColorAutomatic
        .StrikeThrough = False
```

```
                .DoubleStrikeThrough = False
                .Outline = False
                .Emboss = False
                .Shadow = False
                .Hidden = False
                .SmallCaps = False
                .AllCaps = False
                .Color = wdColorAutomatic
                .Engrave = False
                .Superscript = False
                .Subscript = False
                .Spacing = 0
                .Scaling = 100
                .Position = 0
                .Kerning = 0
                .Animation = wdAnimationNone
                .Ligatures = wdLigaturesNone
                .NumberSpacing =
    wdNumberSpacingDefault
                .NumberForm = wdNumberFormDefault
                .StylisticSet =
    wdStylisticSetDefault
                .ContextualAlternates = 0
        End With
    End Sub
```

Apply underline red single formatting to text

Run the macro:
```
    Sub Red_Underline()
    '
    ' Red_Underline Macro
    '
        Selection.Font.UnderlineColor =
    wdColorRed
```

```
End Sub
```

Decrease the font size by 1 point

Run the macro:

```
Sub Decrease_The_Font_Size_By_1_Point()
'
' Decrease_The_Font_Size_By_1_Point Macro
'
    Selection.Font.Size =
Selection.Font.Size - 1
End Sub
```

➡	You can change a number in red circle (below). It means how many font will be smaller.

```
Sub Decrease_The_Font_Size_By_1_Point()
'
' Decrease_The_Font_Size_By_1_Point Macro
'
'
    Selection.Font.Size = Selection.Font.Size - 1
End Sub
```

Increase the font size by 1 point

Run the macro:

```
Sub Increase_The_Font_Size_By_1_Point()
'
' Increase_The_Font_Size_By_1_Point Macro
'
'
    Selection.Font.Size =
Selection.Font.Size + 1
End Sub
```

➡	You can change a number in red circle (below). It means how many font will be bigger.

```
Sub Increase_The_Font_Size_By_1_Point()
'
' Increase_The_Font_Size_By_1_Point Macro
'
'
    Selection.Font.Size = Selection.Font.Size + 1
End Sub
```

Center the text

Run the macro:
```
    Sub Center_The_Text()
    '
    ' Center_The_Text Macro
        Selection.ParagraphFormat.Alignment =
    wdAlignParagraphCenter
    End Sub
```

Align the text to the left

Run the macro:
```
    Sub Align_The_Text_To_The_Left()
    '
    ' Align_The_Text_To_The_Left Macro
    '
        Selection.ParagraphFormat.Alignment =
    wdAlignParagraphLeft
    End Sub
```

Align the text to the right

Run the macro:
```
    Sub Align_The_Text_To_The_Right()
    '
    ' Align_The_Text_To_The_Right Macro
    '
```

```
    Selection.ParagraphFormat.Alignment =
wdAlignParagraphRight
End Sub
```

Cancel a command

Run the macro:
```
Sub Escape_Key()
    '

    ' Escape_Key Macro
        Selection.EscapeKey
End Sub
```

Adjust the zoom magnification

Run the macro:
```
Sub Adjust_The_Zoom_Magnification()
    '

Adjust_The_Zoom_Magnification Macro

ActiveWindow.ActivePane.View.Zoom.Percent
age = 200
End Sub
```

| | You can change a number in red circle (below). It means zoom (200 = 200%). |

```
Sub Adjust_The_Zoom_Magnification()
    '

' Adjust_The_Zoom_Magnification Macro
    '

    '

    ActiveWindow.ActivePane.View.Zoom.Percentage = 200
End Sub
```

Split the document window

Run the macro:

```
Sub Split_The_Document_Window()
'
' Split_The_Document_Window Macro

    ActiveWindow.Panes(2).Activate
    ActiveWindow.SplitVertical = 50
End Sub
```

Remove the document window split

Run the macro:

```
Sub Remove_The_Document_Window_Split()
'
' Remove_The_Document_Window_Split Macro
'
    ActiveWindow.SplitVertical = 100
End Sub
```

Print to PDF

Run the macro:

```
Sub Print_pdf_file()
'
' Print_pdf_file Macro
'
    ActivePrinter = "Microsoft Print to
PDF"
    Application.PrintOut FileName:="",
Range:=wdPrintAllDocument, Item:= _
        wdPrintDocumentWithMarkup,
Copies:=1, Pages:="", PageType:= _
        wdPrintAllPages, Collate:=True,
Background:=True, PrintToFile:=False, _
```

```
                    PrintZoomColumn:=0,
        PrintZoomRow:=0, PrintZoomPaperWidth:=0,

    —
                    PrintZoomPaperHeight:=0
End Sub
```

Move the cursor one word to the right

Run the macro:

```
Sub
Move_The_Cursor_One_Word_To_The_Right()
    '
    ' Move_The_Cursor_One_Word_To_The_Right
Macro
    '
    '

        Selection.MoveRight Unit:=wdWord,
Count:=1
End Sub
```

	You can change a number in red circle (below). This is the number of words the cursor will move to the right.

```
Sub Move_The_Cursor_One_Word_To_The_Right()
    '
    ' Move_The_Cursor_One_Word_To_The_Right Macro
    '
    '

        Selection.MoveRight Unit:=wdWord, Count:=1
End Sub
```

Move the cursor one word to the left

Run the macro:

```
Sub
Move_The_Cursor_One_Word_To_The_Left()
'
' Move_The_Cursor_One_Word_To_The_Left
Macro
'
'

    Selection.MoveLeft Unit:=wdWord,
Count:=1
End Sub
```

➡️ You can change a number in red circle (below). A negative number indicates a shift in the opposite direction.

```
Sub Move_The_Cursor_One_Word_To_The_Left()
'
' Move_The_Cursor_One_Word_To_The_Left Macro
'
'

    Selection.MoveLeft Unit:=wdWord, Count:=(-2)
End Sub
```

Move the cursor up by one paragraph

Run the macro:

```
Sub Move_The_Cursor_Up_By_One_Paragraph()
'
' Move_The_Cursor_Up_By_One_Paragraph
Macro
```

```
'

'

     Selection.MoveUp Unit:=wdParagraph,
Count:=1
End Sub
```

| → | You can change a number in red circle (below). It means number of paragraphs once. A negative number indicates a shift in the opposite direction. |

```
Sub Move_The_Cursor_Up_By_One_Paragraph()
'

' Move_The_Cursor_Up_By_One_Paragraph Macro
'

'

     Selection.MoveUp Unit:=wdParagraph, Count:=1
End Sub
```

Move the cursor down by one paragraph

Run the macro:

```
Sub
Move_The_Cursor_Down_By_One_Paragraph()
'

' Move_The_Cursor_Down_By_One_Paragraph
Macro
'

'

     Selection.MoveDown Unit:=wdParagraph,
Count:=1
End Sub
```

| → | You can change a number in red circle (below). „1" is for one paragraph. |

```
Sub Move_The_Cursor_Down_By_One_Paragraph()
'
' Move_The_Cursor_Down_By_One_Paragraph Macro
'
'
    Selection.MoveDown Unit:=wdParagraph, Count:=1
End Sub
```

Move the cursor to the end of the current line

Run the macro:
```
Sub
Move_The_Cursor_To_The_End_Of_The_Current
_Line()
'
'
Move_The_Cursor_To_The_End_Of_The_Current
_Line Macro
'
'
    Selection.EndKey Unit:=wdLine
End Sub
```

Move the cursor to the beginning the current line

Run the macro:
```
Sub
Move_The_Cursor_To_The_Beginning_The_Curr
ent_Line()
'
'
Move_The_Cursor_To_The_Beginning_The_Curr
ent_Line Macro
```

```
'
'
      Selection.HomeKey Unit:=wdLine
End Sub
```

Move the cursor to the top of the screen

Run the macro:
```
Sub
Move_The_Cursor_To_The_Top_Of_The_Screen(
)
'
'
Move_The_Cursor_To_The_Top_Of_The_Screen
Macro
'
'
      Application.Browser.Previous
End Sub
```

Move the cursor to the bottom of the screen

Run the macro:
```
Sub
Move_The_Cursor_To_The_Bottom_Of_The_Scre
en1()
'
'
Move_The_Cursor_To_The_Bottom_Of_The_Scre
en1 Macro
'
'
```

```
        Selection.HomeKey Unit:=wdWindow
   End Sub
```

Move the cursor by scrolling the document view up by one screen

Run the macro:

```
    Sub
    Move_The_Cursor_By_Scrolling_The_Document
    _View_Up_By_One_Screen()
    '
    '
    Move_The_Cursor_By_Scrolling_The_Document
    _View_Up_By_One_Screen Macro
    '
    '
        Selection.MoveUp Unit:=wdScreen,
    Count:=1
    End Sub
```

> ⇨ You can change a number in red circle (below). „2"
> means two screens once.

```
Sub Move_The_Cursor_By_Scrolling_The_Document_View_Up_By_One_Screen()
'
' Move_The_Cursor_By_Scrolling_The_Document_View_Up_By_One_Screen Macro
'
'
    Selection.MoveUp Unit:=wdScreen, Count:=②
End Sub
```

Move the cursor by scrolling the document view down by one screen

Run the macro:

```
Sub
Move_The_Cursor_By_Scrolling_The_Document
_View_Down_By_One_Screen()
'
'
Move_The_Cursor_By_Scrolling_The_Document
_View_Down_By_One_Screen Macro
'
'
    Selection.MoveDown Unit:=wdScreen,
Count:=1
End Sub
```

> ➡ You can change a number in red circle (below). „3"
> means two screens once.

```
Sub Move_The_Cursor_By_Scrolling_The_Document_View_Down_By_One_Screen()

' Move_The_Cursor_By_Scrolling_The_Document_View_Down_By_One_Screen Macro
'
'
    Selection.MoveDown Unit:=wdScreen, Count:=3
End Sub
```

Move the cursor to the top of the next page

Run the macro:

```
Sub
Move_The_Cursor_To_The_Top_Of_The_Next_Pa
ge()
'
'
Move_The_Cursor_To_The_Top_Of_The_Next_Pa
ge Macro
'
'
    Application.Browser.Next
End Sub
```

⇨	To move twice – see macro below.

```
Sub Move_The_Cursor_To_The_Top_Of_The_Next_Page()
'
' Move_The_Cursor_To_The_Top_Of_The_Next_Page Macro
'
'

    Application.Browser.Next
    Application.Browser.Next

End Sub
```

Move the cursor to the top of the previous page

Run the macro:

```
    Sub
    Move_The_Cursor_To_The_Top_Of_The_Previou
    s_Page()
    '
    '
    Move_The_Cursor_To_The_Top_Of_The_Previou
    s_Page Macro
    '
    '

        Application.Browser.Previous
    End Sub
```

⇨	To move twice – see macro below.

```
Sub Move_The_Cursor_To_The_Top_Of_The_Previous_Page()
'
' Move_The_Cursor_To_The_Top_Of_The_Previous_Page Macro
'
'

    Application.Browser.Previous
    Application.Browser.Previous
End Sub
```

Move the cursor to the end of the document

Run the macro:

```
Sub
Move_The_Cursor_To_The_End_Of_The_Documen
t()
'
'
Move_The_Cursor_To_The_End_Of_The_Documen
t Macro
'
'
    Selection.EndKey Unit:=wdStory
End Sub
```

Move the cursor to the beginning of the document

Run the macro:

```
Sub
Move_The_Cursor_To_The_Beginning_Of_The_D
ocument()
'
'
Move_The_Cursor_To_The_Beginning_Of_The_D
ocument Macro
'
'
    Selection.HomeKey Unit:=wdStory
End Sub
```

Move the cursor to the location of the previous revision

Run the macro:
```
Sub
Move_The_Cursor_To_The_Location_Of_The_Pr
evious_Revision()
'

'

Move_The_Cursor_To_The_Location_Of_The_Pr
evious_Revision Macro
'

'

    Application.GoBack
End Sub
```

Move the focus to commands on the ribbon

In this example „hero" was bold.
Run the macro:
```
Sub Bold()
'

' Bold Macro
'

'

    Selection.Font.Bold = wdToggle
End Sub
```

	To select the active tab on the ribbon, and activate the access keys use **Alt** or **F10** (in picture below). To move to a different tab, use **access keys** or **arrow keys**.

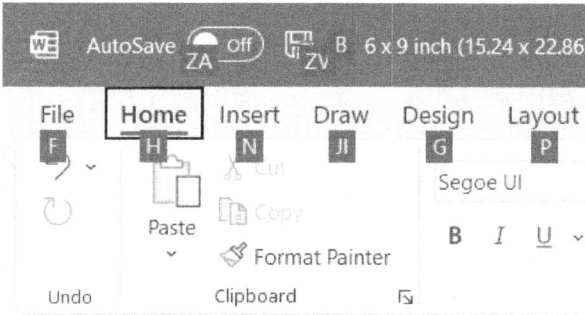

⇒	To move the focus to commands on the ribbon use **Tab** key or **Shift+Tab**.
⇒	To move between command groupings on the ribbon use **Ctrl+Left** or **Right** arrow key.
⇒	To move among the items on the ribbon **arrow key**.

Activate the selected button

In this example „hero" was Zoom 75%.
Run the macro:

```
Sub Button()
'
' Button Macro
'
'

ActiveWindow.ActivePane.View.Zoom.Percentage = 75
End Sub
```

⇒	Activate the selected button use **Spacebar** or **Enter**.

Open the context menu

Run the macro:

```
Sub Context_Menu()
'
' Context_Menu Macro
'
'

    Options.DefaultBorderColor = -
721354753
End Sub
```

> To open the context menu press **Shift+F10** or, on a Windows keyboard, the Context key (between the right **Alt** and right **Ctrl** keys)

Move the cursor one word to the right

Run the macro:

```
Sub Cursor_One_Word_To_The_Right()
'
' Cursor_One_Word_To_The_Right Macro
'
'

    Selection.MoveRight Unit:=wdWord,
Count:=1
End Sub
```

> To move three words – see macro below.

```
Sub Cursor_One_Word_To_The_Right()
'
' Cursor_One_Word_To_The_Right Macro
'
'

    Selection.MoveRight Unit:=wdWord, Count:=3
End Sub
```

Move the cursor one word to the left

Run the macro:

```
Sub Cursor_One_Word_To_The_Left()
'
' Cursor_One_Word_To_The_Left Macro
'
'

    Selection.MoveLeft Unit:=wdWord,
Count:=1
End Sub
```

➡ To move two words – see macro below.

```
Sub Cursor_One_Word_To_The_Left()
'
' Cursor_One_Word_To_The_Left Macro
'
'

    Selection.MoveLeft Unit:=wdWord, Count:=2
End Sub
```

Move the cursor up by one paragraph

Run the macro:

```
Sub Cursor_Up_By_One_Paragraph()
'
' Cursor_Up_By_One_Paragraph Macro
'
'

    Selection.MoveUp Unit:=wdParagraph,
Count:=1
```

```
      End Sub
```

	To move three paragraphs – see macro below.

```
Sub Cursor_Up_By_One_Paragraph()
'
' Cursor_Up_By_One_Paragraph Macro
'
'
    Selection.MoveUp Unit:=wdParagraph, Count: 3
End Sub
```

Move the cursor down by one paragraph

Run the macro:

```
      Sub Cursor_Down_By_One_Paragraph()
      '
      ' Cursor_Down_By_One_Paragraph Macro
      '
      '
          Selection.MoveDown Unit:=wdParagraph,
      Count:=1
      End Sub
```

	To move two paragraphs – see macro below.

```
Sub Cursor_Down_By_One_Paragraph()
'
' Cursor_Down_By_One_Paragraph Macro
'
'
    Selection.MoveDown Unit:=wdParagraph, Count: 2
End Sub
```

Move the cursor to the end of the current line

Run the macro:

```
Sub
Cursor_To_The_End_Of_The_Current_Line()
'
' Cursor_To_The_End_Of_The_Current_Line
Macro
'
'
    Selection.EndKey Unit:=wdLine
End Sub
```

Move the cursor to the beginning of the current line

Run the macro:

```
Sub
Cursor_To_The_Beginning_Of_The_Current_Li
ne()
'
'
Cursor_To_The_Beginning_Of_The_Current_Li
ne Macro
'
'
    Selection.HomeKey Unit:=wdLine
End Sub
```

Move the cursor to the top of the screen

Run the macro:

```
Sub
Move_The_Cursor_To_The_Top_Of_The_Screen(
)
'

'

Move_The_Cursor_To_The_Top_Of_The_Screen
Macro
'

'   Selection.HomeKey Unit:=wdWindow
End Sub
```

Move the cursor to the bottom of the screen

Run the macro:

```
Sub
The_Cursor_To_The_Down_Of_The_Screen()
'

' The_Cursor_To_The_Down_Of_The_Screen
Macro
'

'

    Selection.EndKey Unit:=wdWindow
End Sub
```

Move the cursor by scrolling the document view up by one screen

Run the macro:
```
Sub Up_By_One_Screen()
'
' Up_By_One_Screen Macro
'
'

    Selection.MoveUp Unit:=wdScreen,
Count:=1
End Sub
```

➡️ | To move twenty five screens – see macro below.

```
Sub Up_By_One_Screen()
'
' Up_By_One_Screen Macro
'
'

    Selection.MoveUp Unit:=wdScreen, Count:=25
End Sub
```

Move the cursor by scrolling the document view down by one screen

Run the macro:
```
Sub Down_By_One_Screen()
'
' Down_By_One_Screen Macro
'
```

```
'
    Selection.MoveDown Unit:=wdScreen,
Count:=1
End Sub
```

Print the document

Run the macro:

```
Sub Print_The_Document()
'
' Print_The_Document Macro
'
'

    Application.PrintOut FileName:="",
Range:=wdPrintAllDocument, Item:= _
        wdPrintDocumentWithMarkup,
Copies:=1, Pages:="", PageType:= _
        wdPrintAllPages, Collate:=True,
Background:=True, PrintToFile:=False, _
        PrintZoomColumn:=0,
PrintZoomRow:=0, PrintZoomPaperWidth:=0,
_
        PrintZoomPaperHeight:=0
End Sub
```

Select text right

Run the macro:

```
Sub Select_Text_Right()
'
' Select_Text_Right Macro
' This macro marks 5 characters to the
right of the cursor.
'
    Selection.MoveRight
Unit:=wdCharacter, Count:=5,
Extend:=wdExtend
End Sub
```

Select text left

Run the macro:

```
Sub Select_Text_Left()
'
' Select_Text_Left Macro
' This macro marks 7 characters to the
left of the cursor.
'
    Selection.MoveLeft Unit:=wdCharacter,
Count:=7, Extend:=wdExtend
End Sub
```

Select text up

Run the macro:

```
Sub Select_Text_Up()
'
' Select_Text_Up Macro
'
' This macro marks 8 lines up.
'     Selection.MoveUp Unit:=wdLine,
Count:=8, Extend:=wdExtend
End Sub
```

Select text down

Run the macro:

```
Sub Select_Text_Down()
'
' Select_Text_Down Macro
'
'
' This macro marks 12 lines down.
```

```
     Selection.MoveDown Unit:=wdLine,
Count:=12, Extend:=wdExtend
End Sub
```

Select the word to the left

Run the macro:

```
Sub Select_Word_To_The_Left()
'
' Select_Word_To_The_Left Macro
'
' This macro selects 3 words to the left.
     Selection.MoveLeft Unit:=wdWord,
Count:=3, Extend:=wdExtend
End Sub
```

Select the word to the right

Run the macro:

```
Sub Select_Word_To_The_Right()
'
' Select_Word_To_The_Right Macro
'
' This macro selects 9 words to the
right.
     Selection.MoveRight Unit:=wdWord,
Count:=9, Extend:=wdExtend
End Sub
```

Select text from the current position to the beginning of the current line

Run the macro:

```
Sub
Select_To_The_Beginning_Of_The_Current_Li
ne()
'
Select_To_The_Beginning_Of_The_Current_Li
ne Macro
'
'

    Selection.HomeKey Unit:=wdLine,
Extend:=wdExtend
End Sub
```

Select text from the current position to the end of the current line

Run the macro:

```
Sub
Select_To_The_End_Of_The_Current_Line()
'
' Select_To_The_End_Of_The_Current_Line
Macro
'
'


    Selection.EndKey Unit:=wdLine,
Extend:=wdExtend
End Sub
```

Select text from the current position to the beginning of the current paragraph

Run the macro:

```
Sub
Select_From_The_Current_Position_To_The_B
eginning_Of_The_Current_Paragraph()
'
'
Select_From_The_Current_Position_To_The_B
eginning_Of_The_Current_Paragraph Macro
'
'
    Selection.MoveUp Unit:=wdParagraph,
Count:=1, Extend:=wdExtend
End Sub
```

	To select five paragraphs – see macro below.

```
Sub Select_From_The_Current_Position_To_The_Beginning_Of_The_Current_Paragraph()
'
' Select_From_The_Current_Position_To_The_Beginning_Of_The_Current_Paragraph Macro
'
'
    Selection.MoveUp Unit:=wdParagraph, Count:=5 Extend:=wdExtend
End Sub
```

Select text from the current position to the end of the current paragraph

Run the macro:

```
Sub
Select_From_The_Current_Position_To_The_E
nd_Of_The_Current_Paragraph()
'
'
Select_From_The_Current_Position_To_The_E
nd_Of_The_Current_Paragraph Macro
'
'
    Selection.MoveDown Unit:=wdParagraph,
Count:=1, Extend:=wdExtend
End Sub
```

To select seven paragraphs – see macro below.

```
Sub Select_From_The_Current_Position_To_The_End_Of_The_Current_Paragraph()

' Select_From_The_Current_Position_To_The_End_Of_The_Current_Paragraph Macro
'
    Selection.MoveDown Unit:=wdParagraph, Count:=7, Extend:=wdExtend
End Sub
```

Select from the current position to the top of the screen

Run the macro:

```
    Sub Select_To_The_Top_Of_The_Screen()
    '
    ' Select_To_The_Top_Of_The_Screen Macro
    '
    '
        Selection.MoveUp Unit:=wdScreen,
    Count:=1, Extend:=wdExtend
    End Sub
```

To select twice – see macro below.

```
Sub Select_To_The_Top_Of_The_Screen()
'
' Select_To_The_Top_Of_The_Screen Macro
'
'
    Selection.MoveUp Unit:=wdScreen, Count:=2, Extend:=wdExtend
End Sub
```

Select from the current position to the bottom of the screen

Run the macro:

```
Sub Select_To_The_Bottom_Of_The_Screen()
'
' Select_To_The_Bottom_Of_The_Screen
Macro
'
'
    Selection.MoveDown Unit:=wdScreen,
Count:=1, Extend:=wdExtend
End Sub
```

Select from the current position to the beginning of the document

Run the macro:

```
Sub
Select_To_The_Beginning_Of_The_Document()
'
' Select_To_The_Beginning_Of_The_Document
Macro
'
'
    Selection.HomeKey Unit:=wdStory,
Extend:=wdExtend
End Sub
```

Select from the current position to the end of the document

Run the macro:
```
Sub Select_To_The_End_Of_The_Document()
'
' Select_To_The_End_Of_The_Document Macro
'
'

    Selection.EndKey Unit:=wdStory,
Extend:=wdExtend
End Sub
```

Select from the current position to the bottom of the window

Run the macro:
```
Sub Select_To_The_Bottom_Of_The_Window()
'
' Select_To_The_Bottom_Of_The_Window
Macro
'
'

    Selection.EndKey Unit:=wdWindow,
Extend:=wdExtend
End Sub
```

Delete one word to the left

Run the macro:
```
Sub Delete_One_Word_To_The_Left()
'
' Delete_One_Word_To_The_Left Macro
```

```
'

'

    Selection.Delete Unit:=wdWord,
Count:=-1
End Sub
```

Delete one word to the right

Run the macro:
```
Sub Delete_One_Word_To_The_Right()
'

' Delete_One_Word_To_The_Right Macro
'

'

    Selection.Delete Unit:=wdWord,
Count:=1
End Sub
```

Paste data from the Clipboard task pane

> Office Clipboard allows you to copy and paste content between Microsoft Office apps

Run the macro:
```
Sub Open_The_Clipboard_Task_Pane()
'

' Open_The_Clipboard_Task_Pane Macro
'

'

    Selection.Paste
    Selection.Paste
    Selection.Paste
    Selection.Paste
    Selection.Paste
    Selection.Paste
    Selection.Paste
```

```
        Selection.Paste
        Selection.Paste
        Selection.Paste
        Selection.Paste
        Selection.Paste
    End Sub
```

Cut the selected content to the Clipboard

Run the macro:

```
    Sub Cut()
    '
    ' Cut Macro
    '
    '
        Selection.Cut
    End Sub
```

Copy the selected content to the Clipboard

Run the macro:

```
    Sub Copy()
    '
    ' Copy Macro
    '
    '
        Selection.Copy
    End Sub
```

Paste the contents of the Clipboard

Run the macro:

```
Sub Paste()
'
' Paste Macro
'
'

    Selection.PasteAndFormat
(wdFormatOriginalFormatting)
End Sub
```

Copy the selected formatting

Run the macro:

```
Sub Formatting_Copy()
'
' Formatting_Copy Macro
'
'

    Selection.CopyFormat
End Sub
```

Paste the formatting

Run the macro:

```
Sub Formatting_Paste()
'
' Formatting_Paste Macro
'
'

    Selection.PasteFormat
End Sub
```

Center the paragraph

Run the macro:

```
Sub Center_the_paragraph()
'
' Center_the_paragraph Macro
'
'

    Selection.ParagraphFormat.Alignment =
wdAlignParagraphCenter
End Sub
```

Justify the paragraph

Run the macro:

```
Sub Justify_The_Paragraph()
'
' Justify_The_Paragraph Macro
'
'

    Selection.ParagraphFormat.Alignment =
wdAlignParagraphJustify
End Sub
```

Align the paragraph to the left

Run the macro:

```
Sub Align_The_Paragraph_To_The_Left()
'
' Align_The_Paragraph_To_The_Left Macro
'
'

    Selection.ParagraphFormat.Alignment =
wdAlignParagraphLeft
End Sub
```

Align the paragraph to the right

Run the macro:
```
Sub Align_The_Paragraph_To_The_Right()
'
' Align_The_Paragraph_To_The_Right Macro
'
'

    Selection.ParagraphFormat.Alignment =
wdAlignParagraphRight
End Sub
```

Indent the paragraph

Run the macro:
```
Sub Indent_The_Paragraph()
'
' Indent_The_Paragraph Macro
'
'

    Selection.Paragraphs.Indent
End Sub
```

Remove a paragraph indent

Run the macro:
```
Sub Remove_A_Paragraph_Indent()
'
' Remove_A_Paragraph_Indent Macro
'
'

    Selection.Paragraphs.Outdent
End Sub
```

Create a hanging indent

Run the macro:

```
Sub Create_A_Changing_Indent()
'
' Create_A_Changing_Indent Macro
'
'


Selection.ParagraphFormat.TabHangingInden
t 1
End Sub
```

Remove a hanging indent

Run the macro:

```
Sub Remove_A_Changing_Indent()
'
' Remove_A_Changing_Indent Macro
'
'


Selection.ParagraphFormat.TabHangingInden
t -1
End Sub
```

Remove paragraph formatting

Run the macro:

```
Sub Remove_Paragraph_Formatting()
'
' Remove_Paragraph_Formatting Macro
'
'

    Selection.ParagraphFormat.Reset
End Sub
```

Apply single spacing to the paragraph

Run the macro:

```
Sub
Apply_Single_Spacing_To_The_Paragraph()
'
' Apply_Single_Spacing_To_The_Paragraph
Macro
'
'
    Selection.ParagraphFormat.Space1
End Sub
```

Apply double spacing to the paragraph

Run the macro:

```
Sub
Apply_Double_Spacing_To_The_Paragraph()
'
' Apply_Double_Spacing_To_The_Paragraph
Macro
'
'
    Selection.ParagraphFormat.Space2
End Sub
```

Apply 1.5-line spacing to the paragraph

Run the macro:
```
Sub
Apply_1_and_helf_Line_Spacing_To_The_Para
graph()
'

'

Apply_1_and_helf_Line_Spacing_To_The_Para
graph Macro
'

'

    Selection.ParagraphFormat.Space15
End Sub
```

Add space before the paragraph

Run the macro:
```
Sub Add_Space_Before_The_Paragraph()
'

' Add_Space_Before_The_Paragraph Macro
'

'


Selection.ParagraphFormat.OpenOrCloseUp
End Sub
```

Remove space before the paragraph

Run the macro:
```
Sub Remove_Space_Before_The_Paragraph()
```

```
'
' Remove_Space_Before_The_Paragraph Macro
'
\

    Selection.ParagraphFormat.OpenOrCloseUp
End Sub
```

Enable AutoFormat

Run the macro:
```
Sub Enable_AutoFormat()
'
' Enable_AutoFormat Macro
'
'

    Selection.Document.Kind =
wdDocumentNotSpecified
    Selection.Range.AutoFormat
End Sub
```

Apply the Normal style

Run the macro:
```
Sub Normal_Style()
'
' Normal_Style Macro
'
'

    Selection.Range.Style =
ActiveDocument.Styles(wdStyleNormal)
End Sub
```

Apply the Heading 1 style

Run the macro:
```
Sub Heading_1_Style()
```

```
'
' Heading_1_Style Macro
'
'
    Selection.Style =
ActiveDocument.Styles("Heading 1")
End Sub
```

Apply the Heading 2 style

Run the macro:
```
Sub Heading_2_Style()
'
' Heading_2_Style Macro
'
'
    Selection.Style =
ActiveDocument.Styles("Heading 2")
End Sub
```

Apply the Heading 3 style

Run the macro:
```
Sub Heading_3_Style()
'
' Heading_3_Style Macro
'
'
    Selection.Style =
ActiveDocument.Styles("Heading 2")
End Sub
```

Increase the font size

Run the macro:
```
Sub ICF()
'
```

```
'  ICF Macro
'
'
     Selection.Font.Grow
End Sub
```

Decrease the font size

Run the macro:

```
Sub DCF()
'
'  DCF Macro
'

     Selection.Font.Shrink
End Sub ()
```

Increase the font size by 1 point

Run the macro:

```
Sub ICF1()
'
'  ICF1 Macro
'
'
     Selection.Font.Size =
Selection.Font.Size + 1
End Sub
```

Decrease the font size by 1 point

Run the macro:

```
Sub DCF1()
'
'  DCF1 Macro
'
'
```

```
      Selection.Font.Size =
Selection.Font.Size - 1
End Sub
```

Switch the text between upper case, lower case, and title case

Run the macro:

```
Sub STT()
'
' STT Macro
'
'

    Selection.Range.Case = wdNextCase
    Selection.Range.Case = wdNextCase
    Selection.Range.Case = wdNextCase
End Sub
```

Change the text to all upper case

Run the :

```
Sub UCA()
'
' UCA Macro
'
'

    Selection.Font.AllCaps = wdToggle
End Sub
```

Apply underline formatting to the words, but not the spaces

Run the macro:

```
Sub UBNS()
```

```
'
' UBNS Macro
'
'

    If Selection.Font.Underline =
wdUnderlineWords Then
        Selection.Font.Underline =
wdUnderlineNone
    Else
        Selection.Font.Underline =
wdUnderlineWords
    End If
End Sub
```

Apply double-underline formatting

Run the macro

```
Sub DUF()
'
' DUF Macro
'
'

    If Selection.Font.Underline =
wdUnderlineDouble Then
        Selection.Font.Underline =
wdUnderlineNone
    Else
        Selection.Font.Underline =
wdUnderlineDouble
    End If
End Sub
```

Apply small caps formatting

Run the macro:

```
Sub SC()
'
' SC Macro
```

```
    '
    '
        Selection.Font.SmallCaps = wdToggle
End Sub
```

Apply subscript formatting

Run the macro:
```
Sub subscript()
    '
    ' subscript Macro
    '
    '

        Selection.Font.subscript = wdToggle
End Sub
```

Apply superscript formatting

Run the macro:
```
Sub superscript()
    '
    ' superscript Macro
    '
    '

        Selection.Font.superscript = wdToggle
End Sub
```

Remove manual character formatting

Run the macro:
```
Sub Remove_Formatting()
    '
    ' Remove_Formatting Macro
    '
```

```
'
    Selection.Font.Reset
End Sub
```

Change the selected text to the Symbol font

Run the macro:
```
Sub Symbol()
'
' Symbol Macro
'
'
    Selection.Font.Name = "Symbol"
End Sub
```

Display all nonprinting characters

Run the macro:
```
Sub Nonprinting()
'
' Nonprinting Macro
'
'
    ActiveWindow.ActivePane.View.ShowAll
= Not ActiveWindow.ActivePane.View. _
    ShowAll
End Sub
```

Insert a line break

Run the macro:
```
Sub LB()
'
' LB Macro
```

```
'
'
        Selection.TypeText Text:=Chr(11)
End Sub
```

> More character codes? See Appendix A.

Insert a page break

Run the macro:
```
Sub PB()
'
' PB Macro
'
'

        Selection.InsertBreak
Type:=wdPageBreak
End Sub
```

Insert a column break

Run the macro:
```
Sub CB()
'
' CB Macro
'
'

        Selection.InsertBreak
Type:=wdColumnBreak
End Sub
```

Insert an em dash (—)

Run the macro:
```
Sub EM()
'
' EM Macro
```

```
    '
    '
        Selection.TypeText Text:="—"
End Sub
```

Insert an en dash (–)

Run the macro:
```
    Sub EN()
    '
    ' EN Macro
    '
    '
        Selection.TypeText Text:="–"
End Sub
```

Insert an optional hyphen

Run the macro:
```
    Sub Optional_Hyphen()
    '
    ' Optional_Hyphen Macro
    '
    '
        Selection.TypeText Text:=Chr(31)
End Sub
```

Insert a nonbreaking hyphen

Run the macro:
```
    Sub NH()
    '
    ' NH Macro
    '
    '
        Selection.TypeText Text:=Chr(30)
End Sub
```

Insert a nonbreaking space

Run the macro:

```
Sub NBSP()
'
' NBSP Macro
'
'
    Selection.TypeText Text:=" "
End Sub
```

Insert a copyright symbol (©)

Run the macro:

```
Sub CPR()
'
' CPR Macro
'
'
    Selection.TypeText Text:="©"
End Sub
```

Insert a registered trademark symbol (®)

Run the macro:

```
Sub R()
'
' R Macro
'
'
    Selection.TypeText Text:="®"
End Sub
```

Insert a trademark symbol (™)

Run the macro:

```
Sub TDM()
'
' TDM Macro
'
'
    Selection.TypeText Text:="™"
End Sub
```

Insert an ellipsis

Run the macro:

```
Sub Elipsis()
'
' Elipsis Macro
'
'
    Selection.TypeText Text:="…"
End Sub
```

Move to the next cell in the row and select its content

Run the macro:

```
Sub Next_Cell()
'
' Next_Cell Macro
'
'
    Selection.MoveRight Unit:=wdCell
End Sub
```

Move to the previous cell in the row and select its content

Run the macro:

```
Sub PC()
'
' PC Macro
'
'
    Selection.MoveLeft Unit:=wdCell
End Sub
```

Move to the first cell in the row

Run the macro:

```
Sub First_Cell_In_The_Row()
'
' First_Cell_In_The_Row Macro
'
'
    Selection.HomeKey Unit:=wdRow
End Sub
```

Move to the last cell in the row

Run the macro:

```
Sub Last_Cell_In_The_Row()
'
' Last_Cell_In_The_Row Macro
'
'
    Selection.EndKey Unit:=wdRow
End Sub
```

Move to the first cell in the column

Run the macro:
```
Sub First_Cell_In_The_Column()
'
' First_Cell_In_The_Column Macro
'
'
    Selection.HomeKey Unit:=wdColumn
End Sub
```

Move to the last cell in the column

Run the macro:
```
Sub Last_Cell_In_The_Column()
'
' Last_Cell_In_The_Column Macro
'

    Selection.EndKey Unit:=wdColumn
End Sub
```

Move to the previous row

Run the macro:
```
Sub Previous_Row()
'
' Previous_Row Macro
'
'
    Selection.MoveUp Unit:=wdLine,
Count:=1
End Sub
```

Move to the next row

Run the macro

```
Sub Next_Row()
'
' Next_Row Macro
'
'

    Selection.MoveDown Unit:=wdLine,
Count:=1
End Sub
```

Move one row up

Run the macro

```
Sub One_Row_Up()
'
' One_Row_Up Macro
'
'

    Selection.Range.Relocate wdRelocateUp
End Sub
```

Move one row down

Run the macro

```
Sub One_Row_Down()
'
' One_Row_Down Macro
'
'

    Selection.Range.Relocate
wdRelocateDown
End Sub
```

Select the content in the next cell

Run the macro:

```
Sub Next_Cell1()
'
' Next_Cell1 Macro
'
'

    Selection.MoveRight Unit:=wdCell
End Sub
```

Select the content in the previous cell

Run the macro:

```
Sub Previous_Cell1()
'
' Previous_Cell1 Macro
'
'

    Selection.MoveLeft Unit:=wdCell
End Sub
```

Select a column

Run the macro:

```
Sub Select_A_Column()
'
' Select_A_Column Macro
'
'

    Selection.HomeKey Unit:=wdColumn
    Selection.MoveDown Unit:=wdLine,
Count:=1, Extend:=wdExtend
```

```
End Sub
```

Select a row

Run the macro:

```
Sub Select_A_Row()
'
' Select_A_Row Macro
'
'

    Selection.HomeKey Unit:=wdRow
    Selection.EndKey Unit:=wdRow,
Extend:=True
End Sub
```

Select the whole table

Run the macro:

```
Sub Whole_Table()
'
' Whole_Table Macro
'
'

    Selection.Tables(1).Select
End Sub
```

Insert a new paragraph in a cell

Run the macro:

```
Sub NPIAC()
'
' NPIAC Macro
'
'

    Selection.TypeParagraph
End Sub
```

Insert a tab character in a cell

Run the macro:
```
Sub Tab_In_A_Cell()
'
' Tab_In_A_Cell Macro
'
'
    Selection.TypeText Text:=vbTab
End Sub
```

Insert a comment

Run the macro:
```
Sub Comment()
'
' Comment Macro
'
'
    Selection.Comments.Add
Range:=Selection.Range
    Selection.TypeText Text:="Comment"
End Sub
```

Turn change tracking on or off

Run the macro:
```
Sub Tracking_On()
'
' Tracking_On Macro
'
'
    ActiveDocument.TrackRevisions = Not
ActiveDocument.TrackRevisions
End Sub
```

Insert a DATE field

Run the macro:
```
Sub Insert_Date()
'
' Insert_Date Macro
'
'
    Selection.Fields.Add
Range:=Selection.Range, Type:=wdFieldDate
End Sub
```

Insert a LISTNUM field

Run the macro:
```
Sub Listnum()
'
' Listnum Macro
'
'
    Selection.Fields.Add
Range:=Selection.Range,
Type:=wdFieldListNum, _
        PreserveFormatting:=False
End Sub
```

Insert a PAGE field.

Run the macro:
```
Sub Page()
'
' Page Macro
'
'
    Selection.Fields.Add
Range:=Selection.Range, Type:=wdFieldPage
```

```
End Sub
```

Insert a TIME field

Run the macro:

```
Sub Time()
'
' Time Macro
'
'
    Selection.Fields.Add
Range:=Selection.Range, Type:=wdFieldTime
End Sub
```

Update the linked information in a Microsoft Word source document

Run the macro:

```
Sub Update()
'
' Update Macro
'
'
    Selection.Fields.UpdateSource
End Sub
```

Update the selected fields

Run the macro:

```
Sub Update_Field()
'
' Update_Field Macro
'
'
    Selection.Fields.Update
```

```
End Sub
```

Appendix A. Character codes

From 0 to 127

Code	Character	Code	Character	Code	Character	Code	Character
0		32	[space]	64	@	96	`
1		33	!	65	A	97	a
2		34	"	66	B	98	b
3		35	#	67	C	99	c
4		36	$	68	D	100	d
5		37	%	69	E	101	e
6		38	&	70	F	102	f
7		39	'	71	G	103	g
8	backspace	40	(	72	H	104	h
9	tab	41	)	73	I	105	i
10	linefeed	42	*	74	J	106	j
11	CR	43	+	75	K	107	k
12		44	,	76	L	108	l
13		45	-	77	M	109	m
14		46	.	78	N	110	n
15		47	/	79	O	111	o
16		48	0	80	P	112	p
17		49	1	81	Q	113	q
18		50	2	82	R	114	r
19		51	3	83	S	115	s
20		52	4	84	T	116	t
21		53	5	85	U	117	u
22		54	6	86	V	118	v
23		55	7	87	W	119	w
24		56	8	88	X	120	x
25		57	9	89	Y	121	y
26		58	:	90	Z	122	z
27		59	;	91	[	123	{
28		60	<	92	\	124		
29		61	=	93	]	125	}

30		62	>	94	^	126	~
31		63	?	95	_	127	

CR - carriage return**From 128 to 255**

Code	Character	Code	Character	Code	Character	Code	Character
128	€	160	NBS	192	À	224	à
129		161	¡	193	Á	225	á
130	,	162	¢	194	Â	226	â
131	ƒ	163	£	195	Ã	227	ã
132	„	164	¤	196	Ä	228	ä
133	…	165	¥	197	Å	229	å
134	†	166	¦	198	Æ	230	æ
135	‡	167	§	199	Ç	231	ç
136	^	168	¨	200	È	232	è
137	‰	169	©	201	É	233	é
138	Š	170	ª	202	Ê	234	ê
139	‹	171	«	203	Ë	235	ë
140	Œ	172	¬	204	Ì	236	ì
141		173	SH	205	Í	237	í
142	Ž	174	®	206	Î	238	î
143		175	¯	207	Ï	239	ï
144		176	°	208	Ð	240	ð
145	'	177	±	209	Ñ	241	ñ
146	'	178	²	210	Ò	242	ò
147	"	179	³	211	Ó	243	ó
148	"	180	´	212	Ô	244	ô
149	•	181	µ	213	Õ	245	õ
150	–	182	¶	214	Ö	246	ö
151	—	183	·	215	×	247	÷
152	~	184	¸	216	Ø	248	ø
153	™	185	¹	217	Ù	249	ù
154	š	186	º	218	Ú	250	ú
155	›	187	»	219	Û	251	û
156	œ	188	¼	220	Ü	252	ü
157		189	½	221	Ý	253	ý

158	ž	190	¾	222	Þ	254	þ
159	Ÿ	191	¿	223	ß	255	ÿ

NBS - no-break space; SH - soft hyphen

Index

23007295R00046